I want to be a Pilot

Titles in this series:

I WANT TO BE A

Pilot

DAN LIEBMAN

FIREFLY BOOKS

A FIREFLY BOOK

Published by Firefly Books Ltd. 2018

First Printing, 2018

Library of Congress Control Number: 2018934267

Library and Archives Canada Cataloguing in Publication
Liebman, Daniel, author
      I want to be a pilot / Dan Liebman.
Previously published: Willowdale, Ontario: Firefly Books, 1999.
ISBN 978-0-228-10100-0 (softcover).--ISBN 978-0-228-10144-4 (hardcover)
      1. Air pilots--Juvenile literature. 2. Airplanes--Piloting-- Vocational guidance--Juvenile literature. I. Title. II. Title: Pilot.
TL547.L53 2018   j629.13023   C2018-901063-0

Published in Canada by
Firefly Books Ltd.
50 Staples Avenue, Unit 1
Richmond Hill, Ontario L4B 0A7

Published in the United States by
Firefly Books (U.S.) Inc.
P.O. Box 1338, Ellicott Station
Buffalo, New York, USA 14205

Photo Credits
© Leonard Zhukovsky/Shutterstock.com, front cover
© Dmitry Birin/Shutterstock.com, back cover
© Andrew Park/Shutterstock.com, page 5
© Fasttailwind/Shutterstock.com, page 6
© Sorbis/Shutterstock.com, page 7
© palawat744/Shutterstock.com, pages 8-9
© mTaira/Shutterstock.com, page 10
© Dan Simonsen/Shutterstock.com, page 11, 22–23
© Chris Parypa Photography/Shutterstock.com, pages 12-13
© Yeongsik Im/Shutterstock.com, page 14
© dragunov/Shutterstock.com, page 15
© Aleksandra Suzi/Shutterstock.com, page 16
© Jne Valokuvaus/Shutterstock.com, page 17
© Angelo Giampiccolo/Shutterstock.com, page 18
© Aleksandar Todorovic/Shutterstock.com, page 19
© sirtravelalot/Shutterstock.com, page 20
© Komenton/Shutterstock.com, page 21
© Stokkete/Shutterstock.com, page 24

Design by Interrobang Graphic Design Inc.
Printed and bound in China

Canada   *We acknowledge the financial support of the Government of Canada.*

Some pilots fly small planes. This float plane ties up to a dock – just like a boat does.

Other pilots fly jumbo planes that take people to faraway places.

Large airplanes have many screens and gadgets in front of the pilots. One screen shows how fast the plane is flying.

Two pilots guide their plane down for a landing. Pilots sit in a cabin called the cockpit.

Fighter planes like this one fly high above the clouds. Only very experienced pilots get to fly them.

When planes fly this high, there is not enough air to breathe. That's why the pilot wears a mask with a hose. The hose is connected to an air tank.

The best pilots are sometimes picked to fly at air shows. A group of planes is called a squadron. Air shows are thrilling to watch.

Pilots carry equipment as well as people. The pilot of this helicopter is trained to put out forest fires.

Some helicopters are big enough to carry people long distances. This helicopter can land on water.

It only seems like this pilot is in the sky. He's really on the ground — training to fly at night.

Fighter planes are used in the air force. They have only a small cabin. Pilots must lower themselves down very carefully.

Every airport has a control tower. The people who work in the tower tell pilots when it is safe to take off and to land.

The navigator is part of the air crew. Navigators check the position of the plane in the sky.

There are always new safety rules for pilots to learn.

This pilot is carefully checking his plane before takeoff to make sure it is safe.

Some pilots feel like they are part of the plane. Can you see why?.

It takes a lot of training to be a pilot, but the hard work pays off. For a pilot, every new flight is a new adventure.